AF131391

BOOK ANALYSIS

Written by Ignacio Mayorga Alzate
Translated by Rebecca Neal

Aura

BY CARLOS FUENTES

Bright
≡Summaries.com

CARLOS FUENTES

MEXICAN NOVELIST, SHORT STORY WRITER AND ESSAYIST

- **Born in Panama City in 1928.**
- **Died in Mexico City in 2012.**
- **Literary awards:**
  - Rómula Gallegos International Novel Prize, 1977 (for *Terra Nostra*)
  - Miguel de Cervantes Prize, 1987
  - Prince of Asturias Award for Literature, 1994
- **Notable honours:**
  - Professor of Latin American Literature at Columbia University (1978) and Harvard University (1983)
- **Notable works:**
  - *Where the Air is Clear* (1958), novel
  - *The Death of Artemio Cruz* (1962), novel
  - *Terra Nostra* (1975), novel
  - *The Old Gringo* (1985), novel

Carlos Fuentes was born in Panama on 11 November 1928. His father was a Mexican diplomat, so he lived and went to school in numerous Latin American cities, including Buenos Aires, Santiago and Montevideo, although he spent all his holidays in his parents' homeland. He studied law at the University of Mexico in Mexico City, before moving to Geneva to study economics at the Institute of Advanced International Studies. He began writing at a young age, and worked as a contributing journalist for the magazine *Hoy*. He published his first novel, *Where the Air is Clear*, which is considered to be a key forerunner of the Latin American Boom, in 1958 at the age of 29. In addition to his impressive literary career, which included professorships at prestigious universities such as Columbia and Cambridge, Fuentes was very politically active in Latin American society, and used his writing to reflect on the historical and cultural structures governing life in Mexico.

Fuentes died in 2012, leaving behind a vast body of work comprising essays, novels and short stories. Unlike his contemporaries Gabriel García Márquez (Colombian novelist, 1927-2014) and Mario Vargas Llosa (Peruvian writer, born in 1936), he never received the Nobel Prize in

Literature, but he is nonetheless undoubtedly one of the most important writers of the 20th century not just in Latin America, but in the Spanish-speaking world as a whole. During his lifetime, he received some of the most prestigious honours for Spanish-language writing, including the Mexican National Prize for Arts and Sciences, the Miguel de Cervantes Prize, and the Prince of Asturias Award. His works, which blur the boundaries between history as a discipline and literature as fiction, are an essential landmark in Latin American writing.

AURA

A MEXICAN GOTHIC NOVEL

- **Genre:** Gothic novel/fantastic novel
- **Reference edition:** Fuentes, C. (1986) *Aura*. Trans. Kemp, L. New York: Farrar, Straus and Giroux.
- **1ˢᵗ edition:** 1962
- **Themes:** witchcraft, desire, ritual, duality

Aura is the Mexican writer Carlos Fuentes's fourth novel. It was published in the same year as *The Death of Artemio Cruz*, which is arguably his most influential work, and tells the story of the historian Felipe Montero's encounters with the young Aura and her aunt Consuelo. The titular character's elderly aunt knows that does not have long to live, and tasks Montero with organising her late husband's memoirs. Montero fulfils the functions of both writer and historian, and although his work initially seems mundane, he is soon assailed by mysterious forces that leave him questioning his actions and his sanity.

SUMMARY

FELIPE MONTERO AND THE MYSTERIOUS MANSION

After responding to an advertisement in a local newspaper, Felipe Montero arrives at the mysterious mansion that is home to Consuelo and her niece Aura, who both seem somewhat eccentric. In this gloomy house, he is tasked with organising the memoirs of General Llorente, Consuelo's late husband. Rats have gnawed at the pages of these memoirs, which chronicle Llorente's life in France and his relationship with Consuelo when she was still a young woman. However, Felipe's work is soon interrupted by his burgeoning obsession with the mysterious Aura, who possesses a delicate beauty and is always dressed in green. Before long, he is plunged into a mysterious new reality in which shadows and nightmares guide him through the house's old rooms. The symbolic animals, mystical plants and sinister religious iconography he encounters show him that not everything in the world can be explained by logic and science, and draw him ever deeper into an inescapable alternative reality.

Felipe only spends a few days in Consuelo's mansion. Although he was initially reluctant to grant the old woman's requests, when Aura appears he is so stunned by her beauty and intense green eyes that he changes his mind and falls under the two women's spell. His original motivation for accepting the job was money (his new salary is four times higher than the amount he earned as a teacher), but he soon stops caring about it. He also abandons his plan to pursue his own research alongside his work for Consuelo as Aura takes root in his mind and begins to grow and flourish there like the shadowy garden at the centre of the mansion.

AURA'S SECRET

The mysterious house's two inhabitants share a strange secret. Felipe soon notices that their behaviour is symmetrical: as he sits at the candle-lit table, he observes that Consuelo's actions are exactly the same as Aura's, as if each movement were being reflected by a mirror. The explanation for this is concealed in Llorente's diary, which Felipe reads, rewrites and edits while he is staying at the house. During the course of his work, he discovers all the nuances and hidden facets of Consuelo's personality without even realising he is doing so.

One night, Felipe wakes up from the first dream he has had in a long time to find Aura naked in his room. They sleep together, and the next day Aura invites him back to her room. He is already thinking about freeing her from the clutches of her aunt, whom he believes is holding her captive. Aura tells Felipe that they are married now, and he agrees. The next day, he comes downstairs to find her covered in blood and looking less beautiful than usual as she skins a goat. Meanwhile, Consuelo is in her room and is mirroring Aura's gestures, even though she is not actually skinning an animal. That night, he goes back to Aura's room.

Felipe goes to see Aura in her room after the dinner of kidneys and wine that he has eaten for most meals since he came to the mansion, but she now looks like a middle-aged woman rather than the young girl she was previously. She washes his feet and they embark on a frenzied dance around the room until desire overtakes them and they fall into bed again. When he wakes up, Felipe realises that Consuelo was looking on approvingly the whole time. Aura is now next to her aunt, and both women are once again moving in unison, as if they were a single person.

He is left shaken and confused by this realisation, and asks Aura to explain what is happening. She tells him that Consuelo is going out for the day and that they will talk when they are alone in the house. Consuelo leaves the mansion wearing her tattered wedding gown and Felipe goes back to devouring General Llorente's diaries. He finds out that the young couple could not conceive a child together, which drove Consuelo to begin studying witchcraft. Among the papers, Felipe finds photos of the couple and is dumbfounded when he realises that Consuelo looks identical to Aura and General Llorente looks identical to him. He goes to Consuelo's room, where he discovers that her magic has worked and she and Aura are the same person. He lies down next to her and decides to stay with the elderly woman. Aura will return when Consuelo is strong enough to summon her again.

CHARACTER STUDY

FELIPE MONTERO

Felipe Montero is a 27-year-old Mexican historian who previously studied at the Sorbonne in Paris. When we are introduced to him at the start of the novel, he is sitting in a cheap café in Mexico City. We learn that he is a schoolteacher, but does not find his job fulfilling, as he prefers investigative work that does not require him to move around much. He plans to work on his own book, an ingenious study of the complex interrelated historical processes that Mexico underwent during the colonial era, while he is working for Consuelo.

When he meets Aura, he instantly falls in love with her, becomes convinced that Consuelo is keeping her in the house against her will and begins looking for ways for them to escape together.

CONSUELO LLORENTE

Consuelo is an elderly woman who knows that she does not have long to live, and is looking for a historian to prepare the memoirs of her late husband, General Llorente, for publication. She has an enigmatic way of speaking and is always accompanied by either Aura or Saga, her white rabbit. She appears to be an extremely devout woman and sometimes seems to have mystical visions. She is so old that it is impossible to tell her age by looking at her, her health is fragile and some of her habits (such as dressing in her late husband's military jacket or her tattered wedding dress) are decidedly eccentric. She is a suspicious figure, and as the narrative progresses, it becomes clear that she is hiding a secret from Felipe, and consequently from the novel's readers.

AURA

The titular character is perhaps also the most difficult to pin down. She is enigmatic, smells of the mysterious flowers that she grows in her shadowy garden and is always dressed in green to match her eyes. Her facial features are never fully described, and seem to be constantly changing (when Felipe looks at her, he soon forgets what she looks like and has to look again). Like her elderly aunt, Aura seems to speak in code, and her changing appearance (she sometimes appears as a child and sometimes as an adult woman) seems to conceal just as many secrets.

THE SIGNIFICANCE OF AURA'S NAME

Aura's name can be interpreted in a variety of ways, which all allow us to better understand the novel. Firstly, in Spanish (the language the novel was originally published in), the word can refer to a slight breeze (Mendoza, 2015). This gives us an important insight into her character, because she roams the house like a gentle breeze and brushes against the objects she touches as if she were trying to get lost in the shadows of the ancient mansion. Aura can also mean "a quality or feeling that seems to surround a person or place or to come from them" (*Collins English Dictionary*), but not everybody has one. In this case, it could refer to a kind of magical halo that surrounds the young girl and fascinates Felipe from the day they meet. Finally, and perhaps most importantly, *Cathartes aura* is the Latin name of a species of vulture native to America. Vultures are large, black birds which feed on the carcasses of other animals. They are also associated with witchcraft, which is significant in the context of the novel because this association reinforces the link between Aura and magic. Furthermore, in establishing a connection between his character and an American bird, Fuentes transposes the European tradition of witchcraft to an American context.

ANALYSIS

Genre

Aura is particularly difficult to classify in a single genre. This challenge stems largely from the difficulty of fully understanding the story's female characters. At times, the book appears to be a fantastic novel, with realist elements existing alongside elements associated with fantasy or ghost stories. However, it also contains numerous features of the Gothic novel, particularly in terms of setting: a gloomy house populated by shadows and ghosts, which emerge from the past to inhabit the present and control the future.

Magical realism?

Given the novel's similarities with other works that have been classified as magical realist, it could be argued that it also belongs to this genre. Magical realist works (the best-known of which is arguably Gabriel García Márquez's 1967 novel *One Hundred Years of Solitude*) depict fantastic or bizarre elements within an otherwise realistic setting. In *Aura*, as the story progresses Felipe gradually becomes aware that he has entered a strange, twisted version of reality – a realisation that should make him want to flee the house. However, instead of questioning what he sees, he adapts to it and starts letting his actions be dictated by the house's otherworldly logic: for example, he starts to use his senses of touch and smell to find his way around as the shadows make it impossible to see clearly in the house, and he simply accepts that Aura and Consuelo's movements mirror one another's and that the ages of the two women seem to be constantly changing.

A Gothic novel?

Although the heyday of Gothic fiction came in the 18th and 19th centuries in Europe, these texts influenced many Latin American authors, who incorporated the genre's conventions into their own writing. Novels such as *Aura* and *La casa de las dos palmas* ("The House of the Two Palms", 1988) by Manuel Mejía Vallejo (Colombian writer,

1923-1998) are clear examples of the ways Gothic themes were adapted by Latin American fiction. Although the castles common in European Gothic fiction tend to be situated in remote, shadowy locations, Fuentes's mysterious mansion is in the heart of Mexico City. However, it subverts the rules of the modern city in which is it situated: in stark contrast to the noise of passing buses and ceaseless bustle of the metropolis, it is a shadowy, silent space that immediately strikes the reader as mysterious and unusual. This gloomy, uncanny building draws Felipe, and by extension the reader, into a dark, sinister setting for dark, sinister acts.

Another key characteristic of the Gothic novel is heightened emotion, such as the feelings that overwhelm Felipe when he becomes convinced that Aura is being held against her will by an evil aunt who wants her to stay with her and reminisce about her long-lost youth. Inextricably linked to his desire to rescue her is a latent eroticism: Aura is perceived as a young maiden in danger, and this perception forms the crux of the narrative, as it drives the plot and the decisions that Felipe makes.

A fantastic novel?

Unlike Gothic fiction, fantastic novels are associated with folklore and fairy tales. *Aura* has a significant fantastic dimension which is made obvious right from the epigraph by the French historian Jules Michelet (1798-1874) on the very first page, which mentions "fantasy" and "second sight". This fantastic dimension is associated with the strange acts of witchcraft carried out in Consuelo's house. A closer examination of the rest of the novel reveals numerous allusions to witchcraft (in both its European and American forms) and magic. From the white rabbit that is constantly by Consuelo's side to the scent of plants that surrounds the mysterious Aura, we can identify many symbols associated with witchcraft and the paranormal throughout the novel.

Language and narrative voice

Aura is unusual in that it is written in the second person ("you"): the narrator speaks to the reader as if they know them. Furthermore, it is as though the reader becomes Felipe Montero as they read the novel:

"You're reading the advertisement: an offer like this isn't made every day. You read it and reread it. It seems to be addressed to you and nobody else. [...] All that's missing is your name. The advertisement should have two more words, in bigger, blacker type: Felipe Montero. Wanted, Felipe Montero, formerly on scholarship at the Sorbonne, historian full of useless facts, accustomed to digging among yellowed documents, part-time teacher in private schools [...]. But if you read that, you'd be suspicious and take it as a joke" (pp. 3 and 5).

The tone of the narrative is relatively informal, and the story switches indiscriminately between the present and future tenses, raising the important question of who is actually speaking. Like in Consuelo's house, where individual identities blur into each other, the narrator's identity is left ambiguous. It could be Felipe, who is able to narrate these events in great detail because he has already lived through them, or it could be Consuelo, who is describing the trap that Felipe will fall into and is using her powers of witchcraft to foresee the unsuspecting historian's future.

Fuentes's ingenious approach to constructing his story makes his narrator highly deceptive. The novel's narrative unfolds on two levels simultaneously: on the surface, it seems as though the narrator is simply recounting everything that Felipe is discovering and all the information that makes up the story, but there is more to each event, fact and object than meets the eye, and the story cannot be fully understood until these hidden depths have been revealed. Instead of telling his readers everything that happens, Fuentes tricks the reader by hiding the key elements of the story in plain sight. By the end of the novel, we realise that the clues we needed to understand the mystery surrounding Aura were right in front of us all along, but the narrator's skill meant that they passed by unnoticed.

THEMES

Witchcraft

As we have already explained, *Aura* is filled with references to witches and witchcraft. As such, one of the key clues that allows the mystery of the mansion, and of the story as a whole, to be unravelled is the epigraph by Michelet, as the French historian studied the figure of the witch a century before *Aura* was published. He also examined the relationship between religion, women, nature and fertility, although we are not going to explore this topic in detail in this section.

Witchcraft and nature are closely linked in the novel, as can be seen in the many details making up a complex network of references in the text: Aura always dresses in green, which has been associated with nature since time immemorial; she tends a garden, in which she grows mainly narcotic plants that allow Consuelo to discover the secret of eternal life; the shadowy walls of the house are decorated with bucolic scenes; and Saga the rabbit plays the role of the household deity (a supernatural entity that can be summoned by witches in European folklore and is often associated with fertility). Thanks to her complex relationship with nature, which constitutes a rejection of scientific knowledge, the witch can use magic to continually be reincarnated as her younger double, Aura:

> "Later: "I found her in a delirium, embracing the pillow. She cried 'Yes, yes, yes, I've done it, I've re-created her! I can invoke her, I can give her life with my own life!' It was necessary to call the

doctor. [...]" "[...] Consuelo, my poor Consuelo! Even the devil was an angel once."" (pp. 133 and 135)

When she is unable to conceive a child in the traditional way, Consuelo turns to magic and witchcraft, which her husband considers dangerous. She uses her knowledge of these practices to achieve immortality through Aura, who is repeatedly reborn like the garden she lovingly tends to, or like a fruit, which germinates only to wither away afterwards. Magic also enables Consuelo to bring back her husband in the form of Felipe, who falls so completely under Aura's spell that he gives up his free will and identity to transform into a ghost from the past: General Llorente.

DID YOU KNOW?

Fuentes took the references to magic plants in *Aura* from the same book by Michelet as the epigraph. Michelet's text contains lengthy descriptions of these plant species, and all the plants mentioned are connected to witchcraft. Felipe recognises them because he has read about them in ancient chronicles.

Desire

Magic is used to fulfil desires, and often involves a ritual element: in popular tradition, there are love potions, salves which can cure any ailment and spells to give people superhuman powers. In *Aura*, Consuelo wants to give her husband a child, which would grant her a kind of immortality, since parents live on through their children. In a way, Consuelo is trying to cling to her youth, but she is also trying to bring back her late husband, General Llorente, in the form of the present-day Felipe.

Similarly, Felipe wants to be with Aura and to fulfil his heroic fantasies by saving her from the aunt whom he believes is holding her captive against her will. Felipe justifies his desire by convincing himself that he knows what Consuelo is up to:

> "Now you know why Aura is living in this house: to perpetuate the illusion of youth and beauty in that poor, crazed old lady. Aura, kept here like a mirror, like one more icon on that votive wall with its clustered offerings, preserved hearts, imagined saints and demons" (p. 89)

However, he is mistaken in his assumptions, as it is not Aura who is at the mercy of Consuelo's desires; rather, he is the one who has fallen into her trap and ends up obeying her wishes by staying in the mansion, in a body that is not his own, to satisfy her need for a husband. Seen from another angle, when Felipe fulfils his wish of sleeping with Aura, she projects her own desires onto him and turns him into her husband.

Ritual

In order to fulfil her desire through witchcraft, Consuelo must carry out a ritual, specifically a sacrifice. Before he sleeps with Aura for the first time, Felipe watches cats burning in a fire on the roof (p. 59). This sacrifice is necessary to produce something that goes beyond the results of normal sexual relations: this pagan ritual creates a double, General Llorente, who will inhabit the young historian's body. Furthermore, a passage of the late war hero's memoirs recounts how he found Consuelo naked with her legs spread, torturing a cat before the first time they had sex.

In a second ritual, Felipe loses his own identity for good and turns into the double he has been discovering – and rewriting – since he came to the house. The sacrifice of a goat was a key element of many pagan rituals, so we can see that this scene is central to the novel. Furthermore, this scene reinforces the close link between Consuelo and Aura, as while the young girl is sacrificing the goat in the kitchen, her aunt is carrying out the exact same movements in another room. After this sacrifice (the goat does not form part of the meal that the young historian eats alone later on), Felipe goes to see Aura, who has now taken on the appearance of a middle-aged woman.

The dance, an essential part of the ritual, takes place after Aura symbolically washes Felipe's feet. It starts slowly, before gathering pace and culminating in frenzied physical ecstasy and, inevitably, sexual intercourse. Afterwards, Aura offers Felipe a wafer, which they eat together on the bed they have just had sex on. This subversion of the Catholic communion marks the end of the ritual. It is only after this experience that Felipe notices the duality of Aura and Consuelo.

Duality

Aura is characterised by meticulous symmetry, which only becomes fully apparent after rereading the novel. Specifically, the pairing of Aura and Consuelo is mirrored by the pairing of Felipe and General Llorente. The novel as a whole is permeated by a series of contrasts, which take on significant symbolic connotations.

One such contrast is between the mansion and the city, which are set in complete opposition to one another. Clear contrasts are also present within the house itself: Felipe is given the only well-lit room, as everywhere else is in constant shadow. In metaphorical terms, the contrast between light and darkness represents the opposition between reason and instinct. The light which bathes Felipe's room allows things to be seen as they really are and considered rationally, whereas the gloom of the house's other rooms forces him to use his instincts, senses of touch and smell and animal desires rather than rationality and logic to guide him. Finally, the links between Mexico and France serve a clear purpose: the fact that Mexico is part of the Americas suggests that it is a wild, mystical place, while

France was the birthplace of the Enlightenment, which advocated reason above all else.

Although mirrors invert the images of the objects they reflect, the images they create are undeniably of the same object. With this in mind, Aura and Consuelo's behaviour explains the complex dynamic at the heart of Fuentes's novel. The text is filled with similar connections: for example, immediately after Felipe gives Aura the key to his archives, which contain his life's work, he receives the key to access General Llorente's memoirs. This is a crucial symbolic moment: it represents Felipe's renunciation of his own identity and the beginning of his transformation into his double, which he will only become aware of when he sees the photographs among the pages of Consuelo's late husband's memoirs. Similar examples can be found throughout the book, and may only become apparent on rereading the novel.

FURTHER REFLECTION

SOME QUESTIONS TO THINK ABOUT...

- How does time work in the novel?
- What is the role of the garden in Consuelo's house?
- What is the link between the photograph that Felipe finds and Consuelo's desire?
- Why do you think it is significant that Felipe is a historian?
- What role does religion play in the novel?
- What genre do you think *Aura* belongs to?
- Could anybody else fulfil Felipe's specific role in Consuelo's mansion?
- Who is the novel's narrator? Felipe? Consuelo? Aura? Somebody else? Justify your answer.

We want to hear from you!
Leave a comment on your online library
and share your favourite books on social media!

FURTHER READING

REFERENCE EDITION

- Fuentes, C. (1986) *Aura*. Trans. Kemp, L. New York: Farrar, Straus and Giroux.

REFERENCE STUDIES

- Castañón, A. (2015) Carlos Fuentes: *AURA*. *Carlos Fuentes. Vida y obra*. Bogotá: Norma.

- Mendoza, M. (2015) Un aquelarre en la calle Donceles 815. *Carlos Fuentes. Vida y obra*. Bogotá: Norma.

RECOMMENDED READING

- Michelet, J. (2015) *La Sorciere, the Witch of the Middle Ages*. CreateSpace Independent Publishing Platform.

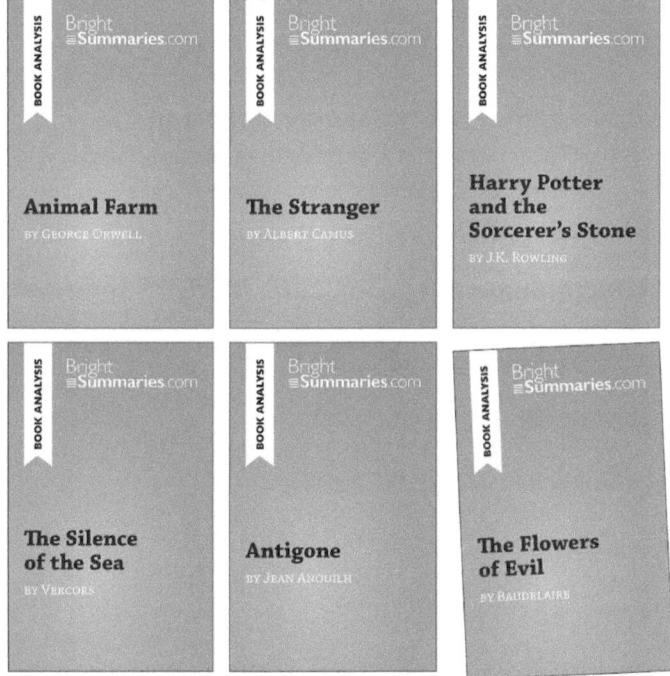

www.brightsummaries.com

Ebook EAN: 9782808002301

Paperback EAN: 9782808008822

Legal Deposit: D/2018/12603/195

Cover: © Primento

Digital conception by Primento, the digital partner of publishers.